Vegan

120 Amazing Vegan Plant-Based Recipes

Written by: Emily Addyson

Copyright © 2017

All rights reserved

All rights reserved. No part of this book may be reproduced or transmitted in any form or by any means, electronic or mechanical, including photocopying, recording or by any information storage and retrieval system, without written permission from the publisher, except for the inclusion of brief quotations in a review.

The author and publisher shall have neither liability or responsibility to anyone with respect to any loss or damage caused, or alleged to be caused, directly or indirectly by the information contained in this book.

Table of Contents

Potato-Kale Hash 7

Chickpea & Greens Crêpe 8

Crêpes With Lemony Cashew Crème 9

Praline Pancakes 10

French Toast 11

Cheesy Grits 12

Curried Mushroom-Tempeh Scramble 13

Asian Vegetable Porridge 14

Beet Tartare 15

Spicy Vegetables 16

Butternut Potage 17

Carrot Bisque 18

Curried Cauliflower Soup 19

Potato-Kale Soup 20

Roasted Corn Chowder 21

Minestrone 22

Barley Soup With Sage 23

Chickpea Chard Stew 24

Split Pea Soup 25

Tunisian Red Lentil Soup 26

Beet Borscht 27

Miso Stew 28

Sesame Noodle Soup 29

Chipotle Spiced Black Bean Soup 30

African Peanut Stew 31

Greek Phyllo Bake 32

Cheese Pasta Pie 33

Nutty Olive Oil Granola 35

Cornmeal Griddle Cakes 36

Avocado Benedict.. 37

Fruit & Oatmeal... 38

Farro Salad 39

Eggplant Salad 40

Mediterranean Artichoke Salad 41

Quinoa & Smoked Tofu Salad 42

Mexican Black Bean Salad 43

Orzo Salad 44

Panzanella 45

Thai Peanut Slaw 46

Bok Choy–Sesame Salad 47

Warm Lentil-Mushroom Salad 48

Barley-Butternut Salad 49

Potato & Smoked Tempeh Salad 51

Kale Caesar 52

Couscous Salad 53

Soba Salad 54

Lentil, Chickpea & Greens Salad 55

Garlic Kale Crostini 56

Red Pepper Hummus... 57

Cauliflower Buffalo Wings 58

Cashew Cheese 59

Tahini Broccoli.. 60

Glazed Butternut Squash 61

Hoisin Green Beans 62

Roasted Brussels Sprouts 63

Cumin-Roasted Carrots 64

Zucchini Fritters 65

Chermoula Eggplant 66

Mushroom Pâté 67

Roman Artichokes 68

Shepherd's Pie 69

Baked Potato Scones 70

Black Currant Scones With Cashew Crème 71

Oats À La Elvis 72

Chia Breakfast Bowl 73

Green Smoothie 74

Chocolate Power Smoothie 75

Cardamom Quinoa Porridge 76

Tofu Scramble 77

Green Chile Chilaquiles 78

Creole Cornbread Bake 79

Italian Tofu Frittata 81

Curried Quinoa-Cauliflower Bake 82

Pea & Pimento Paella 84

Burrito Bake 85

Bread Pudding 86

Chickpea Paella 87

Curry Bowls 88

Mushroom Stroganoff 89

Penne With Garlic Crème 90

Zucchini Primavera 91

Pumpkin-Sage Farfalle 92

Pasta E Fagioli 93

Pasta Bolognese With Lentils 94

Puttanesca Verde 95

Creamy Truffled Linguini	96
Sesame-Peanut Noodles	97
Pad Thai With Tofu	98
Green Mac 'N' Cheese	99
Fusilli With Olives & Raisins	100
Tomato-Caper Pasta	101
Potato Gnocchi With Sage	102
Orzo With Walnuts & Peas	103
Red Pepper Pasta	104
Stuffed Shells	105
Pesto-Olive Pie	106
Curried Potato Pizza	107
Pizza Dough	108
Cashew Crème	109
Tahini-Garlic Dressing	110
Almond Parmesan	111
Peanut Sauce	112
Mushroom Gravy	113
Infused Olive Oil	114
Nacho Sauce	115
Herb Dressing	116
Vinaigrette	117
Creamy Artichoke Pizza	118
Pasta With Vegetables	119
Zesty Pizza	120
Nutty Fudge	121
Rustic Tarte Tatin	122
Chocolate Macaroons	123
Carrot Cake	124

Medjool Truffles 125

Banana Split Parfait 126

Tiramisu 127

Amaretto Mousse 128

Peanut Butter Cookies 129

Mango & Raspberry Parfaits 130

Banana Ice Cream 131

Spinach Pesto 132

POTATO-KALE HASH

extra-virgin olive oil, for sautéing

1 small onion, finely chopped

1 tsp ground cumin

1 garlic clove, minced

1 big sweet potato, peeled & cut right into small dice

1 C. Finely chopped kale

½ C. Water

juice of 1 lemon

salt

freshly ground black pepper

1. In a big nonstick skillet over medium-high heat, add the oil, onion, & cumin. Sauté, stirring for two minutes.

2. Add the garlic, sweet potatoes, & kale. Sauté for two min. More, or till the garlic is fragrant.

3. Add the water. Steam, covered, for five minutes, stirring when or twice, till the potatoes & kale are tender.

4. To serve, squeeze the lemon over the hash. Season with salt & paper.

CHICKPEA & GREENS CRÊPE

½ C. Chickpea flour

1 C. Water

1 tsp extra-virgin olive oil

¼ tsp cumin powder

½ tsp salt

1 C. Chopped spinach, packed

1 scallion, thinly sliced

freshly ground black pepper

1. Heat up the oven to 450°F.

2. In a medium bowl, mix the flour, water, oil, cumin, & salt. Mix to combine, & let the batter rest for a minimum of 1 hour to permit the flavors to marry.

3. Add the chopped spinach & scallion. Mix to combine.

4. Pour the batter right into an oiled pie pan. Bake for 30 minutes, or till the crêpe is golden brown. To serve, dust with pepper.

CRÊPES WITH LEMONY CASHEW CRÈME

¾ C. All-purpose flour

1 tsp baking powder

pinch salt

¾ C. Non-dairy milk

¼ C. Cashew crème

1 Tbsp maple syrup or agave nectar

juice & zest of 1 lemon

coconut oil, for frying

powdered sugar, to garnish

1. In a big bowl, mix the flour, baking powder, salt, & milk. Whisk together till smooth. The batter should be thin.

2. In a small bowl, blend the cashew crème, maple syrup, lemon juice & zest.

3. In a big nonstick skillet over medium-high heat, add a small knob of coconut oil, swirling to cover the pan. Ladle in ¼ of the batter mixture, & cook for 1 to 2 min. On each side. Continue with the remaining batter.

4. To serve, spoon a Tbsp of crème inside each crêpe, spread to cover, & lightly fold right into a cylindrical shape. Garnish with powdered sugar.

PRALINE PANCAKES

¾ C. All-purpose flour

1 tsp baking powder

pinch salt

½ C. Non-dairy milk

½ tsp vanilla extract

½ C. Walnut or pecan halves

¼ tsp ground cinnamon

2 Tbsp maple syrup

coconut oil, for frying

additional maple syrup, to taste

1. Heat up the oven to 400°F.

2. In a big bowl, mix the flour, baking powder, salt, milk, & vanilla. Whisk till smooth.

3. In a small bowl, mix the walnuts, cinnamon, & maple syrup. Spread on a baking sheet & toast in the oven for 3 to 5 minutes, checking after the third min. To prevent burning. Take away from the oven & permit to cool whereas you prepare the pancakes.

4. In a big nonstick skillet, add a knob of coconut oil & ladle in two pancakes-worth of batter. Cook for 2 min. On each side. Continue the process with the remaining batter.

5. To serve, divide the pancakes right into two servings & coat with maple syrup & pralines.

FRENCH TOAST

1 small banana, sliced

2 tsp cornstarch

¾ C. Non-dairy milk

pinch salt

¼ tsp ground cinnamon

4 slices of your favorite bread, sliced in half on the diagonal

2 tsp coconut oil, divided, for frying

maple syrup, for serving

powdered sugar, for serving

1. In a blender, mix the banana, cornstarch, milk, salt, & cinnamon. Purée till smooth.

2. Arrange the bread slices in a casserole dish & cover with the banana-cornstarch mixture, turning when to cover both sides. Let the bread soak up the mixture for 5 minutes.

3. In a nonstick skillet over medium-high heat, add the oil, followed by four of the bread slices.

4. Cook for 3 to 4 min. On each side, or till golden. Repeat with the second batch of bread slices.

5. Serve with maple syrup or a dusting of powdered sugar.

CHEESY GRITS

1¼ C. Water

pinch salt

½ C. Grits

1 tsp vegan margarine

¼ C. Grated vegan cheese, such as daiya

freshly ground black pepper

1. In a small saucepan, mix the water & salt. Bring to a boil.

2. Slowly pour in the grits, stirring constantly.

3. Add the margarine & lower the heat to simmer. Cook for 5 minutes, stirring regularly.

4. When the grits have reached an oatmeal-like consistency, take away from the heat & mix in the grated cheese.

5. Ladle right into bowls, & serve straight away with pepper.

CURRIED MUSHROOM-TEMPEH SCRAMBLE

1 tsp extra-virgin olive oil

1 small onion, finely chopped

1 tsp curry powder

5 cremini or other firm mushrooms, thinly sliced

1 package plain tempeh, chopped right into small dice

¼ C. Finely chopped kale, chard, or other green

1 tsp soy sauce

2 Tbsp water

1. In a medium nonstick skillet over medium-high heat, add the oil & onion. Sauté for 2 minutes, or till onion the becomes fragrant. Add the curry powder & stir.

2. Add the mushrooms & tempeh.

3. Cook, stirring, for 5 minutes, or till the mushrooms shrink to half their size.

4. Add the kale, soy sauce, & water. Mix to combine, lower the heat, & cover. In 5 to 7 minutes, when the water has evaporated & the greens are soft, the scramble is ready to serve.

ASIAN VEGETABLE PORRIDGE

2 C. Water

½ tsp salt

½ C. Cream of rice cereal

1 small turnip, cut right into cubes & steamed

1 scallion, thinly sliced

soy sauce or tamari

toasted sesame oil

1. In a medium saucepan over medium-high heat, bring the water & salt to a boil.

2. Slowly pour in the cereal, stirring with a whisk till well blended.

3. Reduce the heat to low & simmer, stirring constantly, for 1 minute, after which take away from the heat.

4. To serve, ladle the porridge right into bowls. Coat each with half of the turnip, half of the scallions, & a generous drizzle of soy sauce & sesame oil.

BEET TARTARE

4 medium beets, steamed for 20 min. Or till tender & chopped right into small dice

2 tsp freshly squeezed lemon juice

zest of 1 lemon

1 Tbsp extra-virgin olive oil, divided

½ tsp salt

freshly ground black pepper

1 small onion, minced

⅛ tsp smoked paprika

⅛ tsp ground cumin

2 Tbsp chopped Italian parsley

1. In a big bowl, add the beets, lemon juice, lemon zest, 1 tsp oil, salt, & pepper to taste. Let sit for 1 hour to permit the flavors to marry.

2. Strain off the liquid from the beets. In the same bowl, add the onion, paprika, cumin, & remaining 2 tsp oil. Mix to combine.

3. To serve, dash with the parsley. Season with additional salt & pepper.

SPICY VEGETABLES

2 tsp sesame oil

2 cloves garlic, thinly sliced

½-inch piece fresh ginger, minced

2 C. Broccoli florets, washed

½ C. Red cabbage, thinly sliced

½ package tempeh, sliced right into thin strips

½ tsp red pepper flakes

2 Tbsp soy sauce or wheat-free tamari, blended with 2 Tbsp water

1 green onion, washed & thinly sliced

1. In a medium non-stick skillet or wok over medium-high heat, add the sesame oil, garlic, & ginger. Cook, stirring, for 1 minute.

2. Add the broccoli, cabbage, & tempeh, & cook for 3 min. More, stirring constantly.

3. Add the red pepper flakes & soy sauce–water mixture & stir. Cover & lower the heat, & permit to cook for 5 minutes, or till the broccoli & cabbage are tender & the liquid is evaporated.

4. Dash with the green onion slices before serving.

BUTTERNUT POTAGE

1 tsp extra-virgin olive oil

1 small onion, finely chopped

2 garlic cloves, chopped

1 tsp curry powder or paste

1 small butternut squash, peeled, seeded, & cubed

2 C. Water

1 can coconut milk

1 tsp salt

1 tsp sugar

¼ tsp saffron threads, for garnish

1. In a medium saucepan over medium heat, add the oil, onion, garlic, & curry powder. Sauté, stirring, for 2 minutes. Add the squash & sauté 3 min. More.

2. Add the water, & bring to a boil. Reduce the heat & simmer for 15 to 20 minutes, or till the squash is tender.

3. Add the coconut milk, salt, & sugar. Let simmer 5 minutes.

4. Take away from the heat, & utilizing an immersion or standard blender, purée the soup till smooth.

5. Serve warm with the saffron threads as garnish.

CARROT BISQUE

1 tsp extra-virgin olive oil

2 garlic cloves, finely chopped

1 small onion, chopped

1-inch piece fresh ginger, peeled & grated

4 big carrots, chopped right into 1-inch chunks

1 small potato, peeled & cubed

3½ C. Water

3 whole cloves

pinch ground cinnamon

½ tsp salt

freshly ground black pepper

1. In a medium saucepan over medium heat, add the oil, garlic, onions, & ginger. Sauté, stirring, for 5 minutes.

2. Add the carrots, potato, water, cloves, cinnamon, & salt. Simmer, covered, for 15 to 20 minutes, or till the carrots are tender.

3. Take away from the heat.

4. Utilizing a spoon, take away the cloves & discard. Utilizing an immersion blender or standard blender, purée the remaining soup. Return to the pot, heat through, dash with pepper, & serve.

CURRIED CAULIFLOWER SOUP

1 tsp extra-virgin olive oil

½ tsp mustard seeds

1 small onion, chopped

1 garlic clove, minced

1 tsp curry powder

½ cauliflower head, chopped

3 C. Water

1 tsp salt

1 Tbsp tomato paste

juice of 1 lemon

¼ C. Finely chopped cilantro

1. In a medium saucepan over medium-high heat, add the oil & mustard seeds. When they start to pop, add the onion, garlic, & curry powder. Sauté for 2 minutes.

2. Add the cauliflower, water, salt, & tomato paste. Simmer, covered, for 20 minutes, or till the cauliflower is tender.

3. Utilizing an immersion or standard blender, purée the cauliflower mixture. Before serving, mix in the lemon juice & cilantro.

POTATO-KALE SOUP

1 tsp extra-virgin olive oil

1 big onion, peeled & chopped

2 garlic cloves, minced

1 tsp smoked paprika

3½ C. Water

1 big potato, peeled & cubed

1 can cannellini beans

1 tsp salt

2 C. Roughly chopped kale

freshly ground black pepper

1. In a medium saucepan over medium-high heat, add the oil & onion. Sauté, stirring, for 3 minutes.

2. Add the garlic & paprika. Sauté for 1 min. More.

3. Add the water, potato, beans, & salt. Bring to a boil, reduce heat, & simmer, covered, for 20 minutes.

4. Add the kale & simmer, uncovered, for 10 min. More.

5. To serve, ladle right into bowls & dust with pepper.

ROASTED CORN CHOWDER

1 tsp extra-virgin olive oil, divided

2 C. Canned or fresh corn kernels

1 jalapeño pepper, seeded & chopped

1 red bell pepper, seeded & roughly chopped

1 big onion, peeled & chopped

2 garlic cloves, minced

1 big potato, peeled & cubed

2½ C. Water

1 tsp salt

1 C. Soy or coconut milk

freshly ground black pepper

1. Heat up the oven to 450°F.

2. In a small bowl, mix ½ tsp oil, corn, jalapeño pepper, & red bell pepper. Mix to cover with oil.

3. On a baking sheet, spread the corn-pepper mixture & roast in the oven for 15 minutes, turning once. Take away from oven & set aside.

4. In a medium saucepan over medium heat, add the remaining ½ tsp oil, onion, & garlic. Sauté for 3 minutes.

5. Add the potato, water, & salt. Simmer for 15 minutes, or till the potato is tender. Take away from the heat.

6. Add the corn-pepper mixture & milk. Utilizing an immersion or standard blender, purée the mixture, leaving a few chunks for texture. Return to the heat & simmer for 3 minutes. To serve, season with pepper.

MINESTRONE

1 tsp extra-virgin olive oil

1 small onion, diced

2 garlic cloves, minced

1 tsp herbes de provence

3 Tbsp tomato paste

3½ C. Water

1 big carrot, chopped right into small chunks

1 potato, cut right into small chunks

1 tsp salt

1 C. Uncooked macaroni or other small pasta

½ can kidney or cannellini beans

2 C. Chopped spinach

freshly ground black pepper

1. In a big saucepan over medium heat, add the oil, onion, garlic, & herbes de provence. Sauté, stirring, for 3 minutes. Add the tomato paste, water, carrot, potato, & salt. Mix to mix & bring to a boil.

2. Add the uncooked pasta & beans.

3. Reduce the heat & simmer, covered, for 20 minutes.

4. Five min. Before serving, add the spinach & pepper.

BARLEY SOUP WITH SAGE

1 tsp extra-virgin olive oil

1 small onion, finely chopped

1 medium carrot, diced

2 celery stalks, diced

10 cremini or other firm mushrooms, thickly sliced

¼ tsp dried sage

½ C. Pearl barley

4 C. Water

1 bay leaf

1 tsp salt

freshly ground black pepper

1. In a medium saucepan over medium heat, add the oil, onions, carrot, celery, mushrooms, & sage. Sauté for 5 minutes, stirring.

2. Add the barley, water, & bay leaf. Bring to a boil. Reduce the heat & simmer, covered, for 25 to 30 minutes, giving the pot a mix every 10 minutes.

3. Take away the lid, & add salt & pepper to taste.

4. Test the barley for doneness; if it's soft & chewy, the soup is ready.

CHICKPEA CHARD STEW

1 tsp extra-virgin olive oil

1 small onion, chopped

2 garlic cloves, finely chopped

1 tsp smoked paprika

1 can chickpeas

3 C. Finely chopped chard leaves & stems

3 C. Water

2 big tomatoes, roughly chopped

¼ C. Finely chopped Italian parsley

juice from lemon wedges

salt

freshly ground black pepper

1. In a big saucepan over medium heat, add the oil, onion, garlic, & paprika. Sauté, stirring, for 3 minutes. Add the chickpeas. Sauté, stirring, for 3 more minutes.

2. Add the chard & sauté, stirring, for 3 minutes. Add the water & tomatoes. Mix to combine. Lower the heat & simmer, covered, for 20 minutes.

3. Mix in the parsley, ladle right into bowls, & squeeze lemon juice over each one. Season with salt & pepper. Serve warm.

SPLIT PEA SOUP

1 tsp extra-virgin olive oil

1 small onion, chopped

2 garlic cloves, finely chopped

1 tsp smoked paprika

1 carrot, finely chopped

1 jalapeño, poblano, or other hot green pepper, seeded & finely chopped

1½ C. Dried split peas

4 C. Water

1 tsp salt

1. In a medium saucepan over medium heat, add the oil, onion, garlic, & paprika. Sauté, stirring, for 3 minutes. Add the carrot & jalapeño. Sauté, stirring, for 3 more minutes.

2. Add the split peas & water. Stir. Bring to a boil, cover, & reduce the heat. Let simmer 30 minutes, after which mix in the salt.

3. Utilizing an immersion or standard blender, purée the soup & return to the heat. Warm through & serve.

TUNISIAN RED LENTIL SOUP

1 tsp extra-virgin olive oil

1 small onion, finely chopped

2 garlic cloves, minced

1 tsp cumin powder

1 tsp chili powder

1 tsp smoked paprika

½ tsp ground cinnamon

1 tsp salt

freshly ground black pepper

1½ C. Red lentils

3½ C. Water

2 big tomatoes, finely chopped

½ C. Finely chopped cilantro

lemon wedges, for garnish

1. In a medium saucepan over medium-high heat, add the oil & onion. Sauté for 3 minutes. Add the garlic, cumin, chili powder, paprika, cinnamon, salt, & pepper to taste. Cook for an additional minute.

2. Add the lentils, water, & tomatoes. Bring to a boil. Cover, reduce the heat, & cook for 30 minutes, stirring when or twice.

3. Take away from the heat & mix in the cilantro.

4. To serve, squeeze a lemon wedge over the soup & season with pepper.

BEET BORSCHT

1 tsp extra-virgin olive oil

1 small onion, finely chopped

1 garlic clove, quartered

2 big beets, peeled & cut right into dice

1 carrot, cut right into small dice

1 medium potato, peeled & cut right into small dice

1 bay leaf

4 C. Water

¼ C. Finely chopped fresh dill

1 tsp salt

freshly ground black pepper

1 dill pickle, roughly chopped

1. In a medium saucepan over medium heat, add the oil & onion. Sauté for 3 minutes, stirring.

2. Add the garlic, beets, carrot, potato, bay leaf, & water. Bring to a boil, cover, & reduce the heat. Let simmer for 20 minutes.

3. Add the dill, salt, & pepper to taste. Simmer 10 min. More & take away from the heat.

4. To serve, ladle right into bowls & garnish with a heaping tsp of chopped dill pickle.

MISO STEW

3½ C. Water

½-inch fresh ginger piece, peeled & cut right into thin coins

2 garlic cloves, thinly sliced

1 small onion, thinly sliced

5 mushrooms, thinly sliced

1 small potato, peeled & thinly sliced

1 small carrot, thinly sliced

3 Tbsp miso paste

1 C. Roughly chopped spinach

1 tsp sesame oil

1 scallion, thinly sliced

1. In a medium saucepan over medium-high heat, mix the water, ginger, garlic, onion, mushrooms, potato, & carrot. Bring to a boil. Reduce the heat & simmer for 20 minutes, or till the carrots are tender.

2. In a mug, add the miso & ladle in enough of the hot soup broth to dissolve the paste. When the miso is dissolved, pour the broth mixture back in the pot.

3. Add the spinach & take away from the heat.

4. To serve, ladle right into bowls, drizzle with the sesame oil, & coat with scallions.

SESAME NOODLE SOUP

1 tsp sesame oil

1 garlic clove, minced

4 shiitake or other mushrooms, thinly sliced

1-inch piece fresh ginger, peeled & thinly sliced

3 C. Water

3 Tbsp soy sauce or tamari

4 oz. Buckwheat noodles

1 C. Roughly chopped spinach

2 scallions, thinly sliced

1. In a medium saucepan over medium heat, add the sesame oil, garlic, mushrooms, & ginger. Sauté, stirring, for 3 minutes.

2. Add the water & soy sauce. Bring to a boil, add the noodles, & reduce the heat. Simmer 5 minutes.

3. Add the spinach & scallions.

4. Let simmer 2 min. More, after which serve.

CHIPOTLE SPICED BLACK BEAN SOUP

1 small onion, finely chopped

2 garlic cloves, minced

1 red bell pepper, seeded & chopped

1 tsp cumin powder

2 chipotle peppers in adobo sauce, minced

2 cans black beans, drained & rinsed

3 C. Water

salt

¼ C. Chopped fresh cilantro

1 tsp extra-virgin olive oil

1. In a big saucepan over medium-high heat, add the oil, onion, garlic, red bell pepper, & cumin powder. Sauté, stirring, for 3 minutes. Add the chipotle peppers, beans, & water. Simmer for 20 minutes.

2. Utilizing an immersion or standard blender, purée the soup, leaving some whole beans for texture.

3. Season with salt, & garnish with cilantro before serving.

AFRICAN PEANUT STEW

1 tsp extra-virgin olive oil

1 small onion, minced

1 jalapeño pepper, seeded & chopped

1-inch piece fresh ginger, finely chopped

½ tsp curry powder

1 big sweet potato, peeled & cubed

¼ C. Peanut butter

1 can coconut milk

1 big tomato, chopped

2½ C. Water

salt

freshly ground black pepper

1. In a medium saucepan over medium-high heat, add the oil, onion, jalapeño, ginger, & curry powder. Sauté, stirring, for 3 minutes. Add the sweet potato & sauté for 2 min. More.

2. In a small bowl or big measuring cup, mix together the peanut butter & coconut milk. Pour right into the sweet potato mixture & stir.

3. Lower the heat. Add the tomato & water. Simmer, covered, for 20 minutes.

4. Season with salt & pepper. Serve hot.

GREEK PHYLLO BAKE

3 tsp extra-virgin olive oil, divided

1 small onion, finely chopped

1 garlic clove, minced

1 tsp dried oregano

1 C. Cooked du puy lentils

1 C. Chopped spinach

1 tsp salt, divided

4 oz. Tofu, crumbled

juice of 1 lemon

10 black olives, roughly chopped

3 sheets phyllo pastry, trimmed to the size of your baking pan

1. Heat up the oven to 375°F.

2. In a medium nonstick skillet over medium heat, add 1 tsp oil, onion, garlic, & oregano. Sauté, stirring, for 4 minutes. Add the lentils & spinach. Cook for 3 min. More, or till the spinach is wilted but still bright green. Season with ½ tsp salt & take away from the heat.

3. In a small bowl, add the crumbled tofu & lemon juice. Season with the remaining ½ tsp salt, add the olives, & mix to combine.

4. In a small baking pan, spoon in the lentil-spinach mixture. Spoon the tofu-olive mixture over the top. Place one sheet of phyllo pastry over the lentils-and-tofu mixture, & brush lightly with the remaining 2 tsp oil. Repeat with the remaining phyllo.

5. Bake for 20 minutes, or till the coat layer is golden brown.

6. Serve hot or cold.

CHEESE PASTA PIE

for the pasta

1 tsp extra-virgin olive oil

1 small onion, peeled & chopped

1 tsp herbes de provence

1 red bell pepper, seeded & cut right into 1-inch-wide strips

1 zucchini, quartered lengthwise & cut right into ½-inch slices

1 C. Cremini mushrooms or other firm variety, thickly sliced

2 C. Roughly chopped spinach

¼ C. Red wine

2 C. Rigatoni, penne, or ziti pasta, cooked till al dente & cooled

for the cheesy sauce

1 tsp cornstarch dissolved in 1 C. Soy milk

½ C. Nutritional yeast

2 Tbsp tomato paste

1 tsp salt

1 garlic clove, minced

freshly ground black pepper

¼ C. Breadcrumbs

to make the pasta

1. Heat up the oven to 450°F.

2. In a big nonstick skillet over medium-high heat, add the oil, onion, & herbes de provence. Sauté for 3 minutes.

3. Add the bell pepper, zucchini, & mushrooms. Sauté, stirring, for 5 minutes.

4. Add the spinach & red wine , & cook for 1 min. More. Take away from the heat, add the cooked pasta, & lightly mix to combine.

to make the cheesy sauce

1. In a small saucepan over medium heat, add the cornstarch–soy milk mixture, nutritional yeast, tomato paste, salt, garlic, & pepper to taste. Bring to a simmer, stirring, till thickened, about 3 minutes.
2. In a lightly-oiled pie pan or small baking dish, spoon in the pasta-vegetable mixture. Pour the cheesy sauce over, coat with the breadcrumbs, & bake.

NUTTY OLIVE OIL GRANOLA

1 C. Rolled oats

¼ C. Raw pumpkin seeds, hulled

2 Tbsp raw sesame seeds

2 Tbsp dried coconut flakes

2 Tbsp maple syrup

2 Tbsp extra-virgin olive oil

½ tsp ground cinnamon

pinch salt

¼ C. Finely chopped dried apricots or dates

non-dairy milk, for serving

1. Heat up the oven to 350°F.

2. In a big bowl, mix the oats, pumpkin seeds, sesame seeds, coconut flakes, maple syrup, oil, cinnamon, & salt.

3. On a parchment-lined baking sheet, spread the granola mixture & toast for 30 minutes, turning twice, till golden brown.

4. Take away the granola from the oven & permit it to cool.

5. Add the apricots & mix to combine.

6. To serve, divide the granola right into two bowls & douse in your favorite non-dairy milk.

CORNMEAL GRIDDLE CAKES

½ tsp salt

¾ C. Water

¾ C. Fine cornmeal

1 Tbsp extra-virgin olive oil, plus extra for frying

½ C. Seasonal berries

jam or maple syrup, for serving

1. In a medium saucepan over high heat, bring the salt & water to a boil. Steadily pour in the cornmeal, whisking continuously till fully combined.

2. Take away from the heat & mix in the oil, followed by the berries. The consistency should be liquid enough to pour. Add more water if needed to thin.

3. In a big nonstick skillet over medium-high heat, pour a bit of oil, after which ladle in ¼ C. Of batter for each cake. Cook for 3 min. On each side, or till golden.

4. To serve, coat with your favorite jam or maple syrup.

AVOCADO BENEDICT

1 tsp cornstarch dissolved in 1 C. Cold water or soy milk

juice of 1 lemon

¼ C. Nutritional yeast flakes

½ tsp salt

pinch saffron or turmeric for color

freshly ground black pepper

for the benedict base

1 english muffin, split in half

1 garlic clove, halved

4 slices prepared tempeh bacon or other vegan bacon

1 small avocado, halved, pitted, & cut right into thin slices

freshly ground black pepper

smoked paprika

to make the hollandaise sauce

1. In a small saucepan over medium-high heat, add the cornstarch-water mixture, lemon juice, nutritional yeast, salt, & saffron.

2. Bring to a boil, stirring constantly.

3. Reduce the heat & simmer, stirring, for 3 minutes, or till thick & bubbly.

4. Take away from the heat. Set the sauce aside.

to make the benedict base

1. Toast the english muffins till golden brown, & rub each slice with half of a garlic clove.

2. Coat each muffin half with two slices of tempeh bacon & half of the avocado slices.

3. Spoon the hollandaise sauce over each avocado-topped muffin.

4. Garnish with pepper & paprika.

5. Serve immediately.

FRUIT & OATMEAL

1 C. Whole oats

2 C. Water pinch of salt

1 tsp cinnamon

non-dairy yogurt, to taste

maple syrup, to taste

½ C. Seasonal berries or sliced fresh fruit

1 Tbsp sunflower seeds

1. mix the oats, water, & pinch of salt. Cover & cook over medium heat, stirring occasionally, for 10 minutes, or till the oats are soft & most of the water has evaporated.

2. To serve, ladle oatmeal right into bowls, dash with cinnamon, after which coat with yogurt, maple syrup, & fresh berries, after which dash with sunflower seeds.

FARRO SALAD

½ C. Farro

1½ C. Water

1 Tbsp olive oil

½ package marinated tofu, cubed

½ C. Sliced shiitake mushrooms

1 C. Cooked green beans

1. In a saucepan over medium-high heat, mix farro & water. Simmer for 30 minutes, or till tender, draining any remaining liquid, if necessary.

2. Whereas the farro cooks, heat the olive oil in a sauté pan over medium heat. Add the tofu & cook, stirring, till browned on all sides, about 10 minutes.

3. Take away the tofu from the pan & set aside. Add the mushrooms to the pan, & cook for 5 minutes, till lightly browned.

4. Add cooked farro, tofu, mushrooms, & green beans back to the pan, toss together, & cook for two min. Till warmed through.

EGGPLANT SALAD

1 medium eggplant, cut right into thick slices

2 Tbsp extra-virgin olive oil, divided

salt

1 can of chickpeas, drained & rinsed

1 big tomato, roughly chopped

1 small red onion, finely chopped

¼ C. Roughly chopped cilantro

1 tsp dried cumin powder

⅛ tsp ground cinnamon

1 tsp agave nectar

juice of 1 lemon

1. Heat up the oven to 475°F.

2. Arrange the eggplant slices on a baking sheet. Drizzle with 1 Tbsp oil, turning to cover both sides. Season with salt & bake in the oven for 30 minutes, turning when or twice, till tender & golden. When cool, chop the eggplant right into thick chunks.

3. In a big bowl, add the eggplant, chickpeas, tomato, onion, & cilantro.

4. In a small bowl, add the cumin, cinnamon, agave nectar, lemon juice, remaining 1 Tbsp oil, & salt to taste. Whisk to combine, after which pour over the chickpea-eggplant mixture.

5. Mix to combine.

6. Serve & enjoy.

MEDITERRANEAN ARTICHOKE SALAD

2 C. Water

1 C. Bowtie or other pasta

¼ C. Roughly chopped pitted black olives, rinsed

1 can cannellini beans or kidney beans, rinsed & drained

1 can artichoke hearts, drained & roughly chopped

1 small garlic clove, minced

1 Tbsp red wine vinegar

1 Tbsp extra-virgin olive oil

½ tsp dried oregano

salt

freshly ground black pepper

1. In a medium saucepan over high heat, bring the water to a boil. Add the pasta & cook for 5 to 7 minutes, or till al dente. Strain & rinse under cold water to halt the cooking process.

2. In a big bowl, mix the pasta, black olives, beans, & artichoke hearts. Mix to combine.

3. In a small bowl, add the garlic, vinegar, oil, oregano, & salt & pepper to taste. Whisk together till combined, after which pour over the salad-pasta mixture & serve.

QUINOA & SMOKED TOFU SALAD

2 C. Water

1 C. Quinoa

1 Tbsp extra-virgin olive oil

juice of 1 lemon

1 small garlic clove, minced

1 package smoked tofu, cut right into small dice

½ cucumber, peeled, seeded, & diced

1 small red bell pepper, seeded & diced

1 small onion, finely chopped

½ C. Chopped fresh parsley

salt

¼ tsp freshly ground black pepper

1. In a medium saucepan, bring water the to a boil, add the quinoa, & cover. Reduce the heat & let simmer for 15 minutes, or till the water has been absorbed. Take away the lid & let cool.

2. In a small bowl, mix the oil, lemon juice, & garlic. Mix to combine.

3. In a big bowl, add the smoked tofu, cucumber, red bell pepper, onion, & parsley. Pour the dressing over & stir.

4. Add the cooled quinoa & mix to combine.

5. Season with salt & pepper before serving.

MEXICAN BLACK BEAN SALAD

for the salad

1 can black beans, drained & rinsed

1 big tomato, washed & cut right into dice

1 big green bell pepper, finely chopped

1 small jalapeño pepper, minced

1 small onion, minced

1 avocado, pitted, halved, & cubed

corn kernels cut from ear of corn, or about ½ cup

for the vinaigrette

juice of 1 lime

1 Tbsp extra-virgin olive oil

¼ tsp toasted cumin powder

salt

freshly ground black pepper

dash tabasco sauce

½ C. Finely chopped fresh cilantro

to make the salad

in a big bowl, mix to mix all the salad ingredients. Be careful not to bruise the avocado.

to make the vinaigrette

in a small bowl, whisk together the lime juice, oil, cumin, salt, pepper, & tabasco sauce. Pour over the black bean mixture, & stir. Add the cilantro & mix again. Serve immediately.

ORZO SALAD

for the salad

3 C. Water

1 tsp salt

1 C. Orzo

½ can chickpeas, drained & rinsed

1 big tomato, diced

1 small red onion, finely chopped

¼ C. Finely chopped fresh basil leaves

¼ C. Finely chopped Italian parsley

for the vinaigrette

1 Tbsp red wine vinegar

1 Tbsp extra-virgin olive oil

1 tsp agave nectar

salt

freshly ground black pepper

to make the salad

1. In a medium saucepan over medium-high heat, bring the water & salt to a boil & add the orzo. Stir, cover, & reduce the heat. Let simmer for 6 to 8 minutes, or till al dente. Drain, rinse, & cool.

2. In a big bowl, add the orzo, chickpeas, tomatoes, onion, basil, & parsley, & mix to combine.

to make the vinaigrette

1. In a small bowl, whisk together the vinegar, oil, & agave nectar. Season with salt & pepper. Pour over the orzo mixture & mix to combine.

2. Season with additional salt & pepper before serving the salad.

PANZANELLA

for the salad

1 big red bell pepper

2 big tomatoes, roughly chopped

1 Tbsp capers, rinsed & drained

1 small red onion, thinly sliced

¼ C. Roughly chopped fresh basil

2 C. Stale baguette, ciabatta, or other firm white bread, cut right into big cubes

for the vinaigrette

1 Tbsp red wine vinegar

2 Tbsp extra-virgin olive oil

1 small garlic clove, minced

salt

freshly ground black pepper

to make the salad

1. Heat up the oven to 475°F.

2. In the oven, roast the red bell pepper for 15 minutes, or till it collapses & the skin is blistered. Let cool, after which peel, seed, & roughly chop.

3. In a big bowl, add the roasted pepper, tomatoes, capers, onion, basil, & bread cubes.

to make the vinaigrette

1. In a small bowl, whisk together the vinegar, oil, & garlic.

2. Pour the dressing over the salad. Season with salt & black pepper before serving the salad.

THAI PEANUT SLAW

for the slaw

2 C. Thinly sliced red cabbage

½ big cucumber, peeled, seeded, & thinly sliced

1 carrot, washed & grated

1 small red onion, thinly sliced

1 small jalapeño pepper, thinly sliced

¼ C. Finely chopped fresh mint leaves

¼ C. Finely chopped fresh basil leaves

¼ C. Finely chopped fresh cilantro leaves

for the dressing

2 Tbsp peanut butter

2 Tbsp coconut milk

2 tsp soy sauce

juice of 1 lime

1 Tbsp agave nectar

½ tsp red chili paste

to make the slaw

in a big bowl, mix all of the ingredients for the slaw.

to make the dressing

1. In a small bowl, mix together the ingredients for the dressing. If the sauce is too thick to pour, add a bit more coconut milk or water to thin.

2. Pour the dressing over the cabbage mixture & mix to combine.

3. Serve immediately.

BOK CHOY–SESAME SALAD

4 baby bok choy florets, washed, trimmed, & finely sliced

1 small red onion, thinly sliced

4 dried shiitake mushrooms, reconstituted in warm water & thinly sliced

¼ C. Finely chopped fresh basil leaves

¼ C. Finely chopped fresh mint leaves

juice of 1 lime

1 tsp toasted sesame oil

1 Tbsp soy sauce or tamari

freshly ground black pepper

red pepper flakes

1. In a big bowl, mix the bok choy, onion, mushrooms, basil, & mint.

2. In a small bowl, whisk together the lime juice, sesame oil, & soy sauce.

3. Pour over the bok choy mixture. Season with black pepper & red pepper flakes.

4. Let marinate for 15 min. Before serving.

WARM LENTIL-MUSHROOM SALAD

¾ C. Du puy lentils

1 tsp herbes de provence

2½ C. Water

2 Tbsp extra-virgin olive oil, divided

2 C. Thickly sliced cremini, portobello, or other firm mushroom

1 big garlic clove, minced

red pepper flakes

1 Tbsp freshly squeezed lemon juice

salt

freshly ground black pepper

1 C. Arugula

¼ C. Finely chopped Italian parsley

1. In a big saucepan, mix the lentils, herbes de provence, & water. Simmer, covered, for 20 minutes, or till the lentils are tender. Drain any excess water & let cool.

2. In a big nonstick skillet over medium-high heat, add 1 Tbsp oil. Sear the mushrooms till golden, about 15 minutes. Add the garlic & red pepper flakes. Cook 1 min. More.

3. In a big bowl, toss the lentils & mushroom-garlic mixture together. Add the lemon juice & remaining 1 Tbsp oil. Season with salt & pepper. Stir.

4. Only before serving, mix in the arugula & parsley & mix to combine.

BARLEY-BUTTERNUT SALAD

for the salad

1 small butternut squash, peeled, seeded, & cut right into small chunks

1 small red onion, thickly chopped

1 tsp extra-virgin olive oil

salt

1 C. Pearl barley

2 C. Water

2 Tbsp roughly chopped toasted walnuts

¼ C. Roughly chopped Italian parsley

1 C. Baby spinach

for the dressing

1 Tbsp balsamic vinegar

2 Tbsp extra-virgin olive oil

1 garlic clove, minced

salt

freshly ground black pepper

to make the salad

1. Heat up the oven 450°F.

2. Place the squash & onions on a baking tray. Toss with the oil & dash with salt. Roast till the squash is tender & the onions are soft & fragrant, about 20 minutes.

3. In a medium-size saucepan, mix the barley & water. Bring to a boil. Lower the heat, cover, & simmer for 25 minutes, or till the barley is tender. Drain if necessary & let cool.

4. In a big bowl, add the barley, squash-onion mixture, walnuts, parsley, & spinach. Mix to combine.

to make the dressing

in a small bowl, whisk together the vinegar, oil, & garlic. Pour the dressing over the barley-squash mixture, stir, & season with salt & pepper. Serve immediately.

POTATO & SMOKED TEMPEH SALAD

for the salad

3 C. Red potatoes, cubed

1 Tbsp extra-virgin olive oil

1 small red onion, finely chopped

1 package smoked tempeh, cut right into big dice

¼ C. Finely chopped Italian parsley

1 scallion, finely chopped

for the vinaigrette

1 Tbsp extra-virgin olive oil

2 Tbsp balsamic vinegar

1 Tbsp dijon mustard

2 Tbsp maple syrup

salt

freshly ground black pepper

to make the salad

1. Wash the potatoes & steam them for 10 to 12 minutes, or till easily pierced with a fork. Drain & set aside.

2. In a nonstick skillet over medium-high heat, add the oil, onion, & tempeh. Sauté, stirring regularly, for 5 to 7 minutes, or till the tempeh is golden, & the onions are translucent.

3. In a big bowl, add the potatoes, tempeh-onion mixture, parsley, & scallion.

to make the vinaigrette

1. In a small bowl, whisk together the oil, vinegar, mustard, & maple syrup.

2. Pour the dressing over the salad, & mix to combine.

3. Season with salt & pepper. Serve immediately.

KALE CAESAR

for the salad

4 C. Thinly sliced kale

1 small red onion, thinly sliced

¼ C. Thinly sliced black olives

1 avocado, diced

for the caesar dressing

3 Tbsp tahini

juice of 1 lemon

2 tsp soy sauce or tamari

1 garlic clove, minced

2 Tbsp nutritional yeast flakes

freshly ground black pepper

salt

to make the salad

in a big bowl, mix all of the ingredients for the salad.

to make the caesar dressing

1. In a small bowl, whisk together all of the ingredients. It should be thick but pourable. If it's too thick, add water a tsp at a time to reach the right consistency.

2. Pour the caesar dressing over the kale mixture & toss to combine. Season generously with pepper, & salt as needed.

COUSCOUS SALAD

1¾ C. Water

¼ C. Raisins

⅓ tsp salt

2 Tbsp extra-virgin olive oil, divided

1 C. Fine couscous

1 small red onion, finely chopped

1 red bell pepper, chopped right into small dice

½ cucumber, peeled, seeded, & chopped right into small dice

1 Tbsp capers, rinsed

¼ C. Roughly chopped toasted almonds

¼ C. Finely chopped cilantro, mint, or Italian parsley

juice of 1 lemon

1 garlic clove, minced

salt

freshly ground black pepper

1. In a medium saucepan, add the water, raisins, salt, & 1 Tbsp oil. Bring to a boil. Mix in the couscous, & straight away take away from the heat.

2. Let stand, covered, for 5 minutes. Transfer to a big bowl & fluff with a fork. When cool, add the onion, bell pepper, cucumber, capers, almonds, & cilantro.

3. In a small bowl, whisk together the lemon juice, remaining 1 Tbsp oil, & garlic.

4. Pour over the couscous mixture. Mix to combine.

5. Season with salt & pepper, & serve.

SOBA SALAD

for the salad

cooked buckwheat noodles for two people

1 medium carrot, grated

1 small red bell pepper, cored & thinly sliced

2 scallions, thinly sliced

for the vinaigrette

½-inch piece fresh ginger, minced

1 small garlic clove, minced

1 tsp toasted sesame oil

1 Tbsp soy sauce or tamari

2 tsp rice wine vinegar

½ tsp sugar

toasted sesame seeds, to garnish

to make the salad

in a big bowl, toss together all of the ingredients.

to make the vinaigrette

1. In a small saucepan over medium-high heat, add the ginger, garlic, sesame oil, soy sauce, vinegar, & sugar for the vinaigrette. Bring to a boil, after which reduce the heat & simmer for 2 minutes. Take away from the heat & let cool slightly.

2. Pour the warm vinaigrette over the noodle-vegetable mixture & toss to combine. Dash with the sesame seeds before serving.

LENTIL, CHICKPEA & GREENS SALAD

for the salad

1 C. Cooked rice or other grain

½ can of chickpeas, rinsed & drained

1 C. Cooked green beans, sliced lengthwise

1 small red onion, peeled & thinly sliced

5 cremini or other firm mushrooms, thinly sliced

3 sun-dried tomatoes packed in olive oil, sliced thinly

for the dressing

2 Tbsp olive oil

1 Tbsp red wine vinegar

½ tsp herbes de provence

1 tsp salt

½ tsp sugar

1. In a big bowl, mix all the salad ingredients.

2. In a small jar, mix the dressing ingredients & shake vigorously till well-combined.

3. Pour the dressing over the salad mixture, toss to combine, & let sit for 20 min. Before serving.

GARLIC KALE CROSTINI

½ baguette, thickly sliced

3 Tbsp extra-virgin olive oil, divided

salt

freshly ground black pepper

2 garlic cloves, minced

3 C. Kale, destemmed & sliced right into thin strips

½ C. Water

juice of ½ lemon

1. Heat up the oven to 400°F.

2. On a baking sheet, arrange the bread slices & brush with 2 tsp oil. Season with salt & pepper. Bake till light golden brown, about 7 minutes.

3. Take away from the oven to cool.

4. In a big nonstick skillet over medium-high heat, add the remaining 1 tsp oil & garlic. Sauté, stirring till the garlic only changes color, taking care not to overcook.

5. Add the kale & sauté, stirring, for 5 minutes.

6. Add the water, cover, & reduce heat, cooking for 5 min. Or till the water evaporates.

7. Take away from the heat, add the lemon juice, & season with salt & pepper.

8. To serve, coat each slice of toasted baguette with a generous spoonful of kale.

RED PEPPER HUMMUS

1 big red bell pepper

2 baguette slices, cubed

1 small garlic clove

¼ C. Toasted walnut pieces

1 tsp smoked paprika

1 tsp balsamic vinegar

juice of ½ lemon

1 tsp extra-virgin olive oil

¼ C. Water

salt

freshly ground black pepper

1. Heat up the oven to 475°F.

2. Roast the red pepper under the broiler for 10 minutes, turning midway through to blacken each side. When the pepper is charred & the flesh has collapsed, take away from the oven & permit to cool before peeling & removing the stem & seeds.

3. On a baking sheet, toast the baguette cubes in the oven till golden, about 3 to 5 minutes.

4. In a food processor, add the garlic & walnuts. Process for 10 seconds.

5. Add the roasted pepper, toasted baguette cubes, & paprika. Process till smooth, about 10 seconds.

6. Add the vinegar, lemon juice, oil, water, & salt & pepper to taste. Pulse till well blended. If the mixture is too thick, add a bit more water to thin.

7. Let sit for an hour or more before serving to permit flavors to develop.

CAULIFLOWER BUFFALO WINGS

½ C. Water or soy milk

½ C. All-purpose flour

1 tsp garlic powder

salt

freshly ground black pepper

3 C. Cauliflower florets, washed & dried

½ C. Hot sauce

2 tsp vegan margarine, melted

1. Heat up the oven to 450°F.

2. In a big bowl, mix the water, flour, garlic powder, salt & pepper to taste. Whisk to combine. Add the cauliflower florets. Toss with a spoon to cover each piece in the flour mixture.

3. On a baking sheet, spread the cauliflower florets & bake for 15 minutes, after which take away from the oven.

4. In a small bowl, mix the hot sauce & vegan margarine. Spoon over the cauliflower, & return to the oven to bake for 10 more minutes.

5. Serve hot with your favorite dipping sauce.

CASHEW CHEESE

1½ C. Water

1 tsp salt

1 tsp garlic powder

2 tsp agar-agar powder

¾ C. Raw cashews, soaked for three hours, drained, & rinsed

¼ C. Nutritional yeast

1 tsp smoked paprika

juice of ½ lemon

1. In a medium saucepan over medium heat, mix the water, salt, garlic powder, & agar-agar powder. Simmer, whisking, till thickened & the agar is fully dissolved, about 5 minutes.

2. Take away from the heat.

3. In a medium-size bowl, add the cashews, nutritional yeast, paprika, & lemon juice.

4. Add the warm agar mixture, & utilizing an immersion or standard blender, blend till smooth.

5. Pour right into a lightly oiled mold or small bowl. Permit to cool before unmolding & slicing.

TAHINI BROCCOLI

for the broccoli

3 C. Broccoli florets, washed & dried

1 Tbsp extra-virgin olive oil

pinch red pepper flakes

salt

freshly ground black pepper

for the sauce

1 small garlic clove, minced

3 Tbsp tahini

juice of 1 lemon

2 Tbsp water

salt

freshly ground black pepper

to make the broccoli

1. Heat up the oven to 450°F.

2. In a big bowl, add the broccoli, oil, & red pepper flakes. Season with salt & pepper.

3. On a baking sheet, add the broccoli florets & roast for 15 minutes, turning once. The broccoli should be tender & lightly browned.

to make the sauce

1. In a small bowl, add the garlic, tahini, lemon juice, & water. Whisk till well blended. Season with salt & pepper.

2. To serve, plate the broccoli & drizzle with the tahini sauce.

GLAZED BUTTERNUT SQUASH

1 small butternut squash, peeled, seeded, & cut right into thick wedges

3 tsp sesame oil, divided

salt

1 Tbsp miso paste

2 Tbsp water

1 Tbsp maple syrup

1. Heat up the oven to 425°F.

2. In a big bowl, add the squash wedges. Drizzle with 1 tsp sesame oil & toss to coat. Season with salt & arrange the wedges on a cookie sheet. Bake for 20 min. Or till only tender, turning once.

3. In a small saucepan over medium heat, mix the miso paste, water, maple syrup, & remaining 2 tsp sesame oil. Simmer, stirring, till the miso dissolves.

4. Spoon the miso glaze over the squash wedges & return to the oven.

5. Bake for 10 min. More before serving.

HOISIN GREEN BEANS

2 tsp coconut, canola, or extra-virgin olive oil

3 C. Fresh green beans, trimmed & sliced in half

2 garlic cloves, finely chopped

2 Tbsp hoisin sauce

2 Tbsp water

salt

red pepper flakes

1. In a medium-size nonstick skillet over medium-high heat, add the oil & green beans & sauté, stirring, for 3 minutes. Add the garlic. Sauté, stirring, for 3 min. More, or till the garlic is golden.

2. Add the hoisin sauce & water. Cook, stirring, till the beans are tender, about 2 minutes. To serve, season with salt & red pepper flakes.

ROASTED BRUSSELS SPROUTS

3 C. Brussels sprouts, trimmed & sliced right into quarters

1 Tbsp extra-virgin olive oil

1 garlic clove, finely chopped

½ tsp salt

pinch red pepper flakes

freshly ground black pepper

1. Heat up the oven to 400°F.

2. In a big bowl, add the brussels sprouts. Toss with the oil, garlic, salt, & red pepper flakes.

3. Pour the brussels sprouts onto a baking sheet & roast for 30 minutes, till golden on the outside & tender on the inside.

4. To serve, season with additional salt & black pepper.

CUMIN-ROASTED CARROTS

4 big carrots, washed, peeled, & cut right into ½-inch chunks

1½ tsp extra-virgin olive oil

½ tsp cumin seeds

½ tsp salt

1. Heat up the oven to 400°F.

2. In a big bowl, mix the carrots, oil, cumin seeds, & salt. Toss to coat.

3. Pour the carrots onto a baking sheet & roast till lightly caramelized & tender, 35 to 40 minutes, turning once.

4. Serve warm.

ZUCCHINI FRITTERS

1 big zucchini, washed & grated

½ tsp salt

1 Tbsp flaxseed

2 Tbsp water

1 small onion, thinly sliced

1 garlic clove, minced

2 Tbsp all-purpose flour

pinch oregano

1 Tbsp coconut or canola oil

lemon wedges, for garnish

1. On a clean tea towel inside a colander, add the zucchini & dash with salt. Let sit for 10 minutes, after which squeeze to take away as much moisture as possible.

2. In a small bowl, add the flaxseed & water. Mix to combine. Let thicken for 5 minutes.

3. In a medium-size bowl, add the zucchini, flaxseed mixture, onion, garlic, flour, & oregano. Mix to combine, after which form right into six patties.

4. In a big nonstick skillet over medium-high heat, add the oil & the zucchini patties. Fry for 3 to 4 minutes, or till golden. Flip & cook for 3 min. More.

5. Serve with your favorite dipping sauce & a squeeze of lemon.

CHERMOULA EGGPLANT

1 medium eggplant, cut right into ½-inch rounds

1½ tsp salt, divided

1 garlic clove, minced

1 tsp smoked paprika

½ tsp cumin powder

¼ C. Finely chopped cilantro, divided

¼ C. Finely chopped parsley, divided

juice of 1 lemon

2 Tbsp extra-virgin olive oil, divided

1. Heat up the oven to 350°F.

2. On a tea towel, spread the eggplant slices & dash both sides with ½ tsp salt. Let sit for 20 minutes, after which pat dry.

3. In a medium bowl, toss together the garlic, paprika, cumin, 2 Tbsp cilantro & 2 Tbsp parsley, lemon juice, 1 Tbsp oil, & ½ tsp salt. Mix to combine.

4. On a lightly oiled baking sheet, arrange the eggplant slices & bake for 20 to 30 minutes, or till tender. Take away from the oven & let cool.

5. In a medium-size nonstick skillet over medium-high heat, add the remaining 1 Tbsp oil & fry the eggplant two or three at a time till crispy & golden.

6. To serve, mix the chermoula sauce again & spoon it over the eggplant slices.

7. Coat with the remaining 2 Tbsp cilantro & remaining 2 Tbsp parsley, season with the remaining ½ tsp salt, & let sit for 20 min. Before serving.

MUSHROOM PÂTÉ

2 tsp extra-virgin olive oil

½ C. Finely chopped onion

1 garlic clove, minced

3 C. Roughly chopped cremini, portobello, or other firm mushroom

½ tsp herbes de provence

½ tsp salt

freshly ground black pepper

¼ C. Red wine

2 Tbsp nutritional yeast

1 Tbsp miso paste

1 medium waxy potato, peeled, steamed, cooled, & roughly chopped

2 tsp agar-agar powder, dissolved in ½ C. Water

1. In a medium-size nonstick skillet over medium heat, add the oil & onions, stirring occasionally, till the onions are translucent, about 4 minutes. Add the garlic & sauté 1 min. More. Add the mushrooms, herbes de provence, salt, & pepper to taste. Sauté till the mushrooms soften & brown slightly, about 5 minutes.

2. Add the red wine, nutritional yeast, miso, & potato. Mix to combine, after which simmer for 2 minutes. Add the agar-water mixture, stir, & let simmer for 5 min. More.

3. Take away from the heat.

4. Utilizing an immersion blender, purée the mixture whereas still warm.

5. In a lightly oiled mold, add the mushroom mixture.

6. Cool for 20 min. In the fridge before serving.

ROMAN ARTICHOKES

¼ C. Finely chopped parsley

2 garlic cloves, finely chopped

1 tsp salt

2 tsp extra-virgin olive oil

2 big artichokes, washed & trimmed, halved lengthwise, & fuzzy chokes removed

½ C. White wine

½ C. Boiling water

1. Heat up the oven to 450°F.

2. In a small bowl, mix the parsley, garlic, salt, & oil.

3. Place the artichokes in a lightly oiled baking pan. Spoon a dollop of the parsley mixture right into each artichoke half.

4. Slowly pour the wine & water right into the baking dish, taking care not to splash the tops of the artichokes.

5. Cover & bake for 20 to 30 minutes.

6. Let cool slightly before serving.

SHEPHERD'S PIE

2 big potatoes, peeled & roughly chopped

3 C. Water

2 tsp extra-virgin olive oil, divided

1 small onion, finely chopped

1 garlic clove, minced

2 C. Roughly chopped mushrooms

1 tsp salt, divided

1 tsp herbes de provence

1 tsp cornstarch, dissolved in ½ C. Red wine

1 can corn, drained

1. Heat up the oven to 400°F.

2. In a medium saucepan over medium-high heat, add the potatoes & cover with the water. Simmer till tender, about 15 minutes. Drain & cool.

3. In a medium nonstick skillet over medium-high heat, add 1 tsp oil & the onion. Sauté for 3 minutes, after which add the garlic, mushrooms, ½ tsp salt, & herbes de provence. Sauté, stirring, for 5 minutes, after which add the cornstarch-wine mixture. Bring to a simmer, & cook, stirring, for 2 minutes. Take away from the heat.

4. In a medium bowl, add the cooked potatoes, remaining 1 tsp oil, & remaining ½ tsp salt. Utilizing a masher, mash the potatoes to desired consistency.

5. In a lightly oiled pie pan or small baking dish, add the mushroom mixture & pat down to cover the bottom of the pan. Add the corn, & spread to cover the mushroom mixture.

6. Coat the pie off with a layer of mashed potatoes, & bake for 15 to 20 minutes, or till the potatoes are golden.

BAKED POTATO SCONES

¾ C. All-purpose flour

1 tsp baking powder

½ tsp salt

2 Tbsp vegan margarine

¼ C. Grated vegan cheese

1 small potato, peeled, steamed, & mashed

2 Tbsp soy milk

2 scallions, thinly sliced

1. Heat up the oven to 400°F.

2. In a medium bowl, mix the flour, baking powder, & salt.

3. Add the margarine & mix to reach a crumbly consistency, after which add the cheese & mix to combine.

4. In a small bowl, mix the potato, soy milk, & scallions.

5. Add to the flour mixture.

6. On a lightly-floured cutting board, knead the dough till pliable.

7. Shape right into a small circle, after which slice right into four triangles & bake on a lightly oiled baking sheet for 20 minutes. Serve warm.

BLACK CURRANT SCONES WITH CASHEW CRÈME

¾ C. All-purpose flour

1 tsp baking powder

½ tsp salt

2 Tbsp sugar

pinch ground cinnamon

2 Tbsp vegan margarine

2 Tbsp non-dairy milk

2 Tbsp dried currants

zest of 1 lemon

2 Tbsp cashew crème , blended with 1 Tbsp maple syrup

1. Heat up the oven to 400°F.

2. In a medium bowl, mix the flour, baking powder, salt, sugar, & cinnamon.

3. Add the margarine & non-dairy milk. mix till you get a crumbly dough.

4. On a lightly-floured cutting board, knead the dough till pliable, working in the currants & lemon zest a little at a time.

5. Shape the dough right into a small circle.

6. Slice right into four triangles & bake on a lightly oiled baking sheet for 20 minutes.

7. Serve warm with a dollop of cashew crème.

OATS À LA ELVIS

1 ripe banana, mashed

¼ C. Peanut butter

½ tsp ground cinnamon

½ tsp vanilla extract

1 C. Rolled oats

1 C. Non-dairy milk

2 Tbsp maple syrup or agave nectar, divided

1. In a small bowl, mash the bananas & peanut butter to combine.

2. Add the cinnamon, vanilla, oats, & milk & mix to combine.

3. Divide the banana-peanut butter-oat mixture right into two bowls.

4. Coat each bowl with 1 Tbsp of maple syrup.

5. Cover & let sit overnight or for a minimum of 4 hours before serving.

CHIA BREAKFAST BOWL

2 C. Non-dairy milk

½ C. Chia seeds

2 Tbsp shredded, dried coconut

pinch salt

½ tsp vanilla extract

2 Tbsp maple syrup or agave nectar

1 small banana, thinly sliced

1. In a medium-size bowl, mix the non-dairy milk, chia seeds, coconut, salt, vanilla, & maple syrup.

2. Cool overnight.

3. To serve, mix the chia mixture, after which divide right into two bowls.

4. Coat each bowl with sliced banana & extra non-dairy milk if desired.

GREEN SMOOTHIE

2 C. Baby spinach leaves, packed

1 small, ripe avocado, halved, scooped, & chopped

1 ripe pear, cored & chopped

1 Tbsp maple syrup or agave nectar

1 C. Rice milk

1 tsp vanilla extract

1. In a blender, mix all the ingredients & purée till smooth. If the smoothie is too thick, add a bit of water to thin.

2. To serve, pour right into two glasses.

CHOCOLATE POWER SMOOTHIE

1 big banana, sliced

3 medjool dates, pitted

2 Tbsp almond butter

3 Tbsp raw cacao powder

1 tsp flaxseed, finely ground

2 C. Non-dairy milk

½ tsp vanilla extract

pinch salt

add all the ingredients & blend in a high-speed blender till smooth & creamy.

CARDAMOM QUINOA PORRIDGE

1 C. Quinoa

2 C. Non-dairy milk

½ tsp vanilla

⅛ tsp ground cardamom powder

pinch salt

2 Tbsp maple syrup or agave nectar

¼ C. Toasted almonds, roughly chopped

1 ripe nectarine or peach, chopped

1. mix the quinoa, non-dairy milk, vanilla, cardamom, & salt.

2. Cover & cook over low heat, stirring occasionally, for 20 minutes, or till the quinoa expands & turns tender.

3. To serve, ladle right into two bowls.

4. Coat with the maple syrup, chopped nuts, & nectarine.

TOFU SCRAMBLE

1 package of extra-firm tofu, drained & patted dry

salt

freshly ground black pepper

1 tsp chili powder or smoked paprika

1 tsp extra-virgin olive oil

1 small onion, roughly chopped

1 garlic clove, finely chopped

1 small red bell pepper, roughly chopped

corn kernels, freshly scraped from ear of corn

1 small jalapeño pepper, minced

fresh cilantro, for garnish

1. In a big bowl, crumble the tofu & season with salt, pepper, & chili powder.

2. Add the oil to a nonstick skillet.

3. Sauté the onion over medium heat, stirring, for 2 minutes.

4. Add the garlic & cook for one min.

5. Add the tofu, red bell pepper, & corn.

6. Sauté, stirring, for 10 minutes.

7. Mix in the jalapeño, stir, & take away from the heat.

8. To serve, spoon onto plates & garnish with the fresh cilantro.

GREEN CHILE CHILAQUILES

1 Tbsp extra-virgin olive oil

2 corn tortillas, sliced right into thin strips

1 small onion, finely diced

1 package extra-firm tofu, drained, patted dry, & crumbled

1 can chopped green chiles

salt

2 Tbsp water

¼ C. Grated vegan jack-style cheese, such as daiya

squeeze of lime, for garnish

fresh cilantro, for garnish

1. In a big nonstick skillet, heat the oil over medium heat. Add the tortilla slices & onion.

2. Sauté, stirring, for 5 minutes.

3. Add the tofu & green chiles. Season with salt.

4. Sauté for 10 min. More, adding water if necessary to keep the chilaquiles soft & pliable.

5. Take away the chilaquiles from the heat & dash with the grated cheese.

6. To serve, squeeze with lime & dash with cilantro.

CREOLE CORNBREAD BAKE

for the bake

1 small onion, diced

1 tsp extra-virgin olive oil

1 bell pepper, seeded & diced

½ C. Soy curls, covered in hot water

2 garlic cloves, minced

½ tsp cayenne pepper

½ tsp smoked paprika

1 tsp salt

½ tsp freshly ground black pepper

2 big tomatoes, diced

1 C. Fresh okra, sliced right into ¼-inch pieces

corn kernels from 1 ear of corn, or about ½ cup

½ tsp cornstarch, blended with ½ C. Cold water

for the cornbread topping

½ C. Fine yellow cornmeal

½ C. All-purpose flour

1 tsp baking powder

1 tsp sugar

½ tsp salt

1 Tbsp extra-virgin olive oil, coconut oil, or vegan margarine

1 C. Soy milk

2 tsp apple cider vinegar

to make the bake

1. Heat up the oven to 400°F.

2. In a medium-size nonstick skillet over medium-high heat, sauté the onion in oil for 3 minutes. Add the bell pepper & sauté 1 min. More.

3. Drain the soy curls & add them to the skillet along with the garlic, cayenne, paprika, salt, & pepper. Sauté, stirring, for 3 minutes.

4. Add the tomatoes, okra, & corn. Sauté for 2 minutes. Cover with the cornstarch-water mixture, lower the heat, & simmer for 5 minutes.

to make the cornbread topping

1. In a small mixing bowl, whisk together the cornmeal, flour, baking powder, sugar, & salt. Add the oil, soy milk, & vinegar. Whisk well to combine.

2. In a lightly oiled baking pan, add the tomato-okra mixture. Spoon the cornbread mixture on top, & bake for 30 minutes, or till golden.

3. Let cool slightly before serving.

ITALIAN TOFU FRITTATA

½ C. Chickpea flour

1 C. Water

1 tsp salt, divided

1 package extra-firm tofu, rinsed & patted dry

2 Tbsp nutritional yeast

1 tsp oregano or herbes de provence

freshly ground black pepper

5 black olives, pitted & roughly chopped

½ C. Finely chopped Italian parsley

1 C. Roughly chopped spinach, chard, or kale

½ C. Essential marinara

1. In a small bowl, mix the flour, water, & ½ tsp of salt. Mix to mix & let sit for 1 hour or longer.

2. Heat up the oven to 350°F.

3. In a food processor, add the tofu, nutritional yeast, remaining ½ tsp salt, & oregano. Season with pepper & blend till smooth.

4. Transfer the tofu mixture to a big bowl & mix in the olives, parsley, & spinach. Mix to combine, after which pour in the chickpea flour mixture & lightly mix to combine.

5. In a lightly oiled baking dish, spoon in the batter & bake for 45 minutes, or till golden.

6. Slice & serve with a heaping spoonful of essential marinara.

CURRIED QUINOA-CAULIFLOWER BAKE

1 C. Quinoa, rinsed

2 C. Water

1 tsp extra-virgin olive oil or coconut oil

2 tsp curry powder

1 onion, chopped

½ cauliflower head, cut right into small florets

2 big tomatoes, roughly chopped

1 tsp salt

1 big jalapeño or anaheim chile, seeded & chopped

1 can coconut milk

2 Tbsp raisins

¼ C. Raw cashews

¼ C. Chopped fresh cilantro

lemon wedges, for garnish

1. Heat up the oven to 400°F.

2. In a medium saucepan over high heat, bring the quinoa & water to a boil. Reduce heat & simmer for 15 minutes, or till the quinoa has absorbed all the water. Take away from the heat & set aside.

3. In a big nonstick skillet over medium-high heat, add the oil, curry powder, & onion. Sauté, stirring, for 3 minutes. Add the cauliflower florets & cook for 3 min. More.

4. Add the chopped tomatoes, salt, jalapeño, coconut milk, & raisins. Mix to combine, & take away from the heat. Add the quinoa, & mix lightly to combine.

5. In a lightly oiled baking dish, pour the quinoa-cauliflower mixture. Dash the cashews over the top, & bake for 20 minutes, or till the nuts are golden.

6. To serve, plate, & coat with fresh cilantro & a squeeze of lemon.

PEA & PIMENTO PAELLA

2 tsp extra-virgin olive oil

1 small onion, minced

1 small red bell pepper, cut right into thin strips

1 small zucchini, cut lengthwise & thinly sliced

1 tsp smoked paprika

2 Tbsp tomato paste

pinch saffron

juice of ½ lemon

¼ C. Water

1 tsp salt

½ C. Fresh or frozen peas

1½ C. Cooked white rice

10 black or green olives, pitted

4 frozen, canned, or jarred artichoke hearts, halved

¼ C. Chopped Italian parsley

1. In a big nonstick skillet or wok, add the oil & onion & sauté 3 minutes. Add the red bell pepper, zucchini, & paprika. Sauté for 5 min. More, stirring.

2. Add the tomato paste, saffron, lemon juice, water, & salt. Bring to a simmer, after which add the peas, rice, olives, & artichoke hearts. Mix to combine, & let cook for 3 min. More, or till the water is absorbed.

3. To serve, garnish with a generous sprinkling of Italian parsley.

BURRITO BAKE

1½ C. Cooked brown or white rice

1 can black beans or pinto beans, drained & rinsed

1 flour tortilla , cut right into thin strips

5 black olives, pitted & thinly sliced

1 can green or red enchilada sauce

1 scallion, thinly sliced

1 tomato, roughly chopped

1 avocado, halved & seeded

lime wedges

1. Heat up the oven to 400°F.

2. In a lightly oiled baking dish, add the brown rice, pressing to evenly cover the bottom of the pan. Add the beans, & spread to cover the rice. Coat with the tortilla strips & olives, after which smother in the enchilada sauce.

3. Bake for 30 minutes, or till bubbly & slightly browned on top.

4. To serve, garnish each serving with a sprinkling of scallion, half the tomato, half the avocado, & squeeze with fresh lime juice.

BREAD PUDDING

1½ Tbsp extra-virgin olive oil

1 small onion, minced

1 garlic clove, minced

1 tsp herbes de provence

3 C. Stemmed & roughly chopped kale

½ baguette, thickly sliced & cut right into cubes

1 tsp cornstarch, dissolved in 1 C. Soy milk

½ tsp salt

1 tsp dijon mustard

¼ C. Nutritional yeast

⅛ tsp grated nutmeg

freshly ground black pepper

1. Heat up the oven to 400°F.

2. In a big nonstick skillet over medium-high heat, add the oil & onion. Sauté, stirring, for 3 minutes. Add the garlic, herbes de provence, & kale. Cook, stirring, for 5 min. More. Mix in the bread cubes, & cook for an additional 3 minutes. Take away from the heat.

3. In a small saucepan over medium heat, add the cornstarch–soy milk mixture, salt, mustard, nutritional yeast, & nutmeg. Simmer, stirring, for 4 minutes.

4. Take away from the heat.

5. In a lightly oiled baking pan, spoon in the bread mixture & pour the sauce over.

6. Bake for 20 minutes, or till the bread is golden brown, & dust with pepper before serving.

CHICKPEA PAELLA

2 tsp olive oil

1 small onion, minced

2 C. Green beans, washed, trimmed, & sliced in half lengthwise

1 small red bell pepper, washed & sliced right into thin strips

1 tsp smoked paprika

2 Tbsp tomato paste

1 pinch saffron

1 Tbsp lemon juice

¼ C. Water

salt

1 can chickpeas, rinsed & drained

1½ C. Cooked white rice

¼ C. Italian parsley, chopped

1. In a big non-stick skillet or wok, add the olive oil & onion & sauté 3 minutes. Add the green beans, red bell pepper, & smoked paprika & sauté for 5 min. More, stirring.

2. Add the tomato paste, saffron, lemon juice, water, & salt. Bring to a simmer, after which add the chickpeas & rice. Mix to combine, & let cook for 3 min. More, or till the water is absorbed. To serve, garnish with a generous sprinkling of Italian parsley.

CURRY BOWLS

1 Tbsp vegetable oil

½ yellow onion, thinly sliced

1 carrot, thinly sliced

1½ tsp red curry paste

1 tsp freshly grated ginger

2 C. Vegetable broth

1 C. Coconut milk

½ C. Broccoli florets

1 C. Firm tofu, cubed

4 oz. Rice noodles

2 tsp chopped scallions

1. In a medium saucepan over medium heat, add the oil, onion, carrot, curry paste, & ginger. Sauté, stirring, for 5 minutes, till the onions start to brown & the carrot softens slightly.

2. Add the vegetable broth & coconut milk, & bring to a simmer.

3. Add the broccoli & tofu, & simmer for 3 minutes.

4. Add the rice noodles, simmer for 4 minutes, after which take away from heat.

5. Serve garnished with scallions.

MUSHROOM STROGANOFF

1 tsp extra-virgin olive oil

1 small onion, thinly sliced

1 garlic clove, minced

½ tsp smoked paprika

2 C. Thinly sliced cremini, portobello, or other firm mushrooms

¼ C. Red wine

¼ C. Non-dairy yogurt

cooked fettucini for 2 people

salt

freshly ground black pepper

¼ C. Chopped Italian parsley

1. In a big nonstick skillet over medium heat, add oil the & onion. Sauté for 3 minutes. Add the garlic & paprika & sauté 2 min. More.

2. Add the mushrooms & cook, stirring, for 5 minutes. Pour in the red wine, & let simmer for 3 minutes.

3. Add the non-dairy yogurt & fettucini. Mix to combine.

4. To serve, season with salt & pepper. Dash with the parsley.

PENNE WITH GARLIC CRÈME

2 tsp extra-virgin olive oil

3 garlic cloves, minced

1 can white beans, rinsed & drained

1 C. Non-dairy milk

1 tsp salt

cooked penne noodles for 2 people

freshly ground black pepper

pinch red pepper flakes

1. In a big nonstick skillet over medium heat, add the oil & garlic. Cook for 3 minutes. Add the beans & sauté, stirring, for 2 minutes.

2. Utilizing an immersion or standard blender, purée the bean-garlic mixture, non-dairy milk, & salt together till smooth. Return the sauce to the pan & simmer for 2 minutes.

3. Add the penne to the pot, mix to coat, & take away from the heat.

4. Serve with pepper & red pepper flakes.

ZUCCHINI PRIMAVERA

2 big tomatoes

2 garlic cloves, halved

½ tsp salt

1 tsp extra-virgin olive oil

2 medium zucchini, sliced right into thin ribbons with a potato peeler

5 black olives, roughly chopped

1 scallion, thinly sliced

1. In a medium bowl, mix the tomatoes, garlic, salt, & oil. Utilizing an immersion or standard blender, purée till smooth.

2. Add the zucchini ribbons to the tomato-garlic sauce.

3. Add the olives & scallions. Toss to combine.

PUMPKIN-SAGE FARFALLE

1 small pumpkin, butternut, or other firm squash, peeled & cut right into cubes

1 small onion, roughly chopped

3 garlic cloves, quartered

1 Tbsp fresh sage, or 2 tsp dried

2 Tbsp extra-virgin olive oil, divided

1 tsp salt

cooked farfalle noodles for 2 people

freshly ground black pepper

1. Heat up the oven to 400°F.

2. In a big bowl, add the squash, onion, garlic, & sage. Drizzle with 1½ Tbsp oil & mix to combine. Pour the mixture onto a baking sheet, season with the salt, & bake for 30 minutes.

3. In a big bowl, add the cooked noodles & remaining ½ Tbsp oil. Take away the squash mixture from the oven & toss in with the noodles, stirring to combine.

4. Season with pepper. Serve immediately.

PASTA E FAGIOLI

2 tsp extra-virgin olive oil

1 carrot, finely chopped

1 small onion, finely chopped

2 garlic cloves, minced

1 tsp herbes de provence

1 can tomato purée

¼ C. Red wine

¼ C. Water

1 tsp salt

1 can cannellini beans, rinsed & drained

cooked tubetti, macaroni, or other small noodles for 2 people

2 C. Chopped spinach, kale, or chard

freshly ground black pepper

Italian bread, for serving

1. In a big saucepan over medium-high heat, add the oil, carrot, & onion. Sauté for 3 minutes. Add the garlic & herbes de provence. Sauté for 3 min. More.

2. Add the tomato purée, wine, water, & salt. Simmer, stirring, for 10 minutes. Add the beans, noodles, & greens & mix to combine. Let simmer for 5 min. More.

3. Season with pepper & serve with crusty Italian bread.

PASTA BOLOGNESE WITH LENTILS

1 tsp extra-virgin olive oil

1 small zucchini, grated

1 small carrot, grated

½ C. Cooked du puy lentils

1 C. Essential marinara

cooked noodles of choice for 2 people

salt

freshly ground black pepper

1. In a medium saucepan over medium heat, add the oil, zucchini, & carrot. Sauté for 3 minutes. Add the lentils & essential marinara. Simmer, stirring, for 3 minutes.

2. To serve, plate the pasta & spoon the warm sauce over. Season with salt & pepper.

PUTTANESCA VERDE

1 Tbsp extra-virgin olive oil

1 Tbsp capers, rinsed

3 garlic cloves, minced

½ C. Pitted green olives, roughly chopped

2 scallions, thinly sliced

pinch red pepper flakes

2 C. Roughly chopped spinach

cooked spaghetti for 2 people

¼ C. Roughly chopped fresh basil

½ tsp salt

1. In a big nonstick skillet over medium-high heat, add the oil, capers, & garlic. Sauté, stirring, for 3 minutes, after which add the olives, scallions, & red pepper flakes. Cook, stirring, for 3 min. More.

2. Add the spinach & sauté for 1 minute, or till the spinach is soft but still bright green.

3. Add the spaghetti & toss to combine. Only before serving, mix in the basil & season with salt.

CREAMY TRUFFLED LINGUINI

1 tsp extra-virgin olive oil

1 small onion, finely chopped

1 garlic clove, minced

2 C. Roughly chopped mushrooms

2 tsp cornstarch, dissolved in 1 C. Non-dairy milk

2 Tbsp nutritional yeast

1 tsp salt

cooked linguini for 2 people

freshly ground black pepper

1 tsp truffle oil

1. In a medium nonstick skillet over medium heat, add the oil & onion. Cook, stirring, for 3 minutes. Add the garlic & cook 2 min. More.

2. Add the mushrooms & sauté, stirring, for 5 minutes.

3. Add the cornstarch-milk mixture, nutritional yeast, & salt. Simmer, stirring, till thick & bubbly, about 4 minutes.

4. Mix in the linguini & season with pepper.

5. To serve, plate & drizzle each serving with ½ tsp of the truffle oil.

SESAME-PEANUT NOODLES

2 tsp sesame oil

1 garlic clove

½-inch piece fresh ginger, peeled & minced

2 scallions, thinly sliced

1 C. Roughly chopped spinach or bok choy

cooked spaghetti for 2 people

1 tsp sugar, agave, or maple syrup, dissolved in 2 Tbsp soy sauce or tamari

2 Tbsp chopped peanuts

1. In a medium saucepan over medium heat, add the sesame oil, garlic, ginger, & scallions. Sauté, stirring, for 2 minutes.

2. & the spinach & sauté for 2 min. More.

3. Add the spaghetti & toss to combine, after which pour in the sugar-soy sauce mixture. Only before serving, mix in the chopped peanuts.

PAD THAI WITH TOFU

1 tsp peanut, coconut, or canola oil

½ package tofu, drained, patted dry, & chopped right into cubes

¼ C. Peanut butter, mixed with ¼ C. Water

1 tsp red chili sauce

juice of 1 lime

1 tsp sugar, agave, or maple syrup, dissolved in 2 Tbsp soy sauce or tamari

cooked rice noodles for 2 people

¼ C. Chopped fresh cilantro

1 scallion, chopped

lemon or lime wedges, for garnish

1. In a big saucepan over medium-high heat, add the oil & tofu & sauté, stirring, for 5 minutes. Lower the heat & mix in the peanut butter–water mixture, chili sauce, lime juice, & sugar–soy sauce mixture. Add the rice noodles & cilantro. Mix to combine.

2. To serve, garnish with the scallion & a squeeze of lemon or lime juice.

GREEN MAC 'N' CHEESE

1 tsp extra-virgin olive oil

1 small onion, chopped

1 garlic clove, minced

½ tsp ground cumin

2 tsp cornstarch, dissolved in 1 C. Non-dairy milk

¼ C. Nutritional yeast

1 tsp salt 1 can chopped green chiles

cooked macaroni for 2 people

1. In a big nonstick skillet over medium heat, add the oil & onion. Sauté for 3 minutes. Add the garlic & cumin & sauté 2 min. More.

2. Add the cornstarch-milk mixture, nutritional yeast, & salt. Simmer, stirring, for 4 minutes.

3. Add the chiles & noodles. Stir.

4. Serve immediately.

FUSILLI WITH OLIVES & RAISINS

2 tsp extra-virgin olive oil

1 small onion, thinly sliced

2 garlic cloves, thinly sliced

1 small eggplant, cubed

1 tsp herbes de provence

3 Tbsp tomato paste

1 C. Water

¼ C. Raisins

¼ C. Red or green olives, pitted & chopped

cooked fusilli for 2 people

1 tsp salt

¼ C. Roughly chopped Italian parsley

1. In a big nonstick skillet over medium-high heat, add the oil, onion, garlic, eggplant, & herbes de provence. Sauté for 5 minutes.

2. Add the tomato paste, water, raisins, & olives. Mix to combine.

3. Cover, lower the heat, & simmer for 10 minutes.

4. To serve, spoon over the fusilli, season with the salt, & dash with parsley.

TOMATO-CAPER PASTA

2 tsp extra-virgin olive oil

3 garlic cloves, minced

2 C. Cherry tomatoes, sliced in half

1 Tbsp roughly chopped capers

1 Tbsp red wine vinegar

cooked spaghetti for 2 people

¼ C. Finely chopped fresh basil

salt

freshly ground black pepper

1. In a medium nonstick skillet over medium-high heat, add the oil & garlic. Sauté for 2 minutes. Add the cherry tomatoes, capers, & vinegar. Stir.

2. Reduce the heat, cover, & simmer for 5 minutes.

3. To serve, add the cooked spaghetti & basil to the pan. Mix to combine. Season with salt & pepper.

POTATO GNOCCHI WITH SAGE

1 big sweet potato, baked & cooled, skin removed

½ tsp salt

¾ C. All-purpose flour

1 Tbsp extra-virgin olive oil, plus 1 teaspoon, divided

¼ C. Chopped fresh sage leaves

1 garlic clove, minced

1. Bring a big pot of salted water to a boil, after which reduce to a simmer.

2. In a medium bowl, mix the sweet potato, salt, flour, & 1 tsp oil. Mix lightly to combine.

3. On a floured work surface, knead the sweet potato dough for 30 seconds, after which roll right into a cylindrical shape. Slice right into ½-inch-long sections, & lightly press each gnocchi piece with a fork on each side.

4. Lightly slide the gnocchi right into the simmering water. They will straight away sink to the bottom. Cover, & cook for 3 minutes, after which take away the lid. The gnocchi will be floating on coat now. Simmer, cooking, for 2 to 3 min. More, after which lightly drain & rinse with cold water to halt the cooking process.

5. In a big nonstick skillet over medium heat, add the remaining 1 Tbsp oil, sage, & garlic. Cook, stirring, for 2 minutes.

6. Add the gnocchi & sauté for 1 minute, or till the gnocchi is warmed through & coated with sage oil. Serve immediately.

ORZO WITH WALNUTS & PEAS

1 tsp extra-virgin olive oil

1 small onion, minced

1 garlic clove, minced

1½ C. Cooked orzo pasta

¼ C. Frozen peas

¼ C. Non-dairy milk

1 tsp salt

freshly ground black pepper

¼ C. Toasted walnut pieces

¼ C. Finely chopped Italian parsley

1. In a medium nonstick skillet over medium-high heat, add the oil & onion. Sauté for 3 minutes.

2. Add the garlic & cook for 2 min. More.

3. Add the orzo to the pan & stir, followed by the peas, milk, & salt, & season with pepper.

4. Cook, stirring, for 3 minutes, or till the peas are done & the milk has evaporated.

5. Only before serving, mix in the walnuts & Italian parsley.

RED PEPPER PASTA

2 big red bell peppers, roasted, peeled, seeded, & cut right into chunks

2 garlic cloves, minced

1 tsp smoked paprika

2 tsp extra-virgin olive oil

½ tsp salt

cooked rigatoni for 2 people

1 scallion, thinly sliced

almond parmesan

1. In a food processor, pulse the red peppers with the garlic, paprika, oil, & salt.

2. In a medium saucepan over medium heat, add the red pepper mixture & simmer for 5 minutes.

3. Add the pasta & mix to coat.

4. To serve, dash with the scallion & dust with almond parmesan.

STUFFED SHELLS

½ package firm tofu, rinsed & squeezed dry between two tea towels

1 tsp dried oregano

½ tsp salt

1 Tbsp nutritional yeast

1 tsp extra-virgin olive oil

2 garlic cloves, minced

3 C. Roughly chopped fresh spinach

juice of ½ lemon

cooked jumbo pasta shells for 2 people, or about 8 shells

1 C. Of essential marinara

cashew crème

1. Heat up the oven to 400°F.

2. In a big bowl, crumble the tofu right into small pieces. Add the oregano, salt, & nutritional yeast.

3. In a medium nonstick skillet over medium-high heat, add the oil & garlic. Sauté for 2 minutes. Add the spinach & sauté for 2 minutes, or till the spinach is wilted & the liquid has evaporated.

4. Spoon the spinach-garlic mixture right into the tofu & add the lemon juice. Mix to combine, after which stuff each shell generously with the mixture.

5. In a small baking dish, spoon in 3 Tbsp of essential marinara & spread to cover the bottom. Lightly place the stuffed shells on top, after which spoon the remaining sauce over the top. Cover with foil & bake for 15 minutes, after which take away & bake 10 min. More.

6. To serve, add a dollop of cashew crème.

PESTO-OLIVE PIE

1 20-minute pizza dough

3 Tbsp spinach pesto

1 zucchini, thinly sliced

10 olives, thinly sliced

extra-virgin olive oil, for drizzling

salt

freshly ground black pepper

red pepper flakes

almond parmesan

1. Heat up the oven to 425°F.

2. Roll the 20-minute pizza dough out onto a lightly oiled pizza pan.

3. Spread the pesto evenly over the dough.

4. Arrange the zucchini slices over the pesto, followed by the olives. Drizzle with oil & season with salt & pepper.

5. Bake on the coat rack of the oven for 30 minutes.

6. To serve, dust with red pepper flakes & dash with almond parmesan.

CURRIED POTATO PIZZA

1 20-minute pizza dough

3 Tbsp cashew crème

1 tsp curry powder

1 big potato, peeled, thinly sliced, & steamed till tender

1 small onion, thinly sliced

10 olives, thinly sliced

extra-virgin olive oil for drizzling

salt

red pepper flakes

⅓ C. Fresh cilantro leaves

lemon wedges

1. Heat up the oven to 425°F.

2. Roll the 20-minute pizza dough out onto a lightly oiled pizza pan.

3. In a small bowl, mix the cashew crème & curry powder. Spread the mixture evenly over dough.

4. Arrange the potato slices over the cashew crème, followed by the onion slices & olives. Drizzle with oil & season with salt & red pepper flakes.

5. Bake on the coat rack of the oven for 30 minutes.

6. To serve, dash with the cilantro & a squeeze of lemon.

PIZZA DOUGH

1 Tbsp active dry yeast

1 tsp sugar

1 C. Hot water

1 tsp salt

2 C. All-purpose flour

1 Tbsp extra-virgin olive oil

1. In a medium bowl, add the yeast & sugar. Pour in the hot water & let sit for two minutes, or till the mixture begins to froth.

2. Add the salt & flour & mix till the dough becomes firm. Knead by hand in the bowl for 1 min. & shape right into a soft ball.

3. In a big bowl, add the oil. Add the ball of dough & turn in the oil to coat.

4. Let the dough rise for 15 minutes, or till doubled in size, after which punch down right into an additional ball.

5. Press the dough right into a lightly-oiled pizza pan.

6. Heat up the oven to 450°F.

7. Add sauce & toppings of choice.

8. Bake on the middle rack of the oven for 20 minutes, or till the crust turns a golden brown.

CASHEW CRÈME

1 C. Raw cashews

2 C. Water, for soaking, plus ¼ cup

pinch salt

1. In a medium bowl, add the cashews & 2 C. Water. Cover, & let soak for a minimum of 4 hours, or overnight.

2. Drain & rinse the cashews.

3. In a blender or food processor, add the cashews & salt. Blend, adding water as needed to reach a smooth & creamy consistency.

TAHINI-GARLIC DRESSING

2 garlic cloves, minced

2 tsp soy sauce or wheat-free tamari

3 Tbsp tahini

juice of ½ lemon

½ tsp herbes de provence

1. In a small bowl, add the garlic, soy sauce, tahini, lemon juice, & herbes de provence. Whisk together by hand or with an immersion blender. If the sauce is too thick, add a little water to thin.

2. Serve straight away or cool till ready to use.

ALMOND PARMESAN

½ C. Raw almonds or walnuts

1 Tbsp nutritional yeast

½ tsp garlic powder

½ tsp salt

1. In a food processor, add the almonds, nutritional yeast, garlic powder, & salt. Pulse till you reach a crumbly texture.

2. Store in a cool, dry place. The parmesan will stay fresh for up to a month.

PEANUT SAUCE

2 garlic cloves, minced

½ in. Piece fresh ginger, peeled & grated

3 Tbsp peanut butter

3 Tbsp coconut milk

2 tsp soy sauce or wheat-free tamari

juice of ½ a lime

pinch red pepper flakes

1. In a small saucepan over medium heat, add the garlic, ginger, peanut butter, coconut milk, soy sauce, lime juice, & red pepper flakes.

2. Simmer, stirring, for 2 minutes.

3. Serve immediately.

MUSHROOM GRAVY

1 Tbsp extra-virgin olive oil

1 small onion, minced

1 garlic clove, minced

½ tsp dried sage

1 C. Chopped mushrooms

1 Tbsp cornstarch, dissolved in 1 C. Red wine

2 Tbsp nutritional yeast

1 tsp salt

freshly ground black pepper

½ C. Water

1. In a medium nonstick skillet over medium heat, add the oil & onions. Sauté, stirring, for 5 minutes, or till the onions are translucent & soft. Add the garlic & sage. Cook, stirring, for 2 min. More.

2. Add the mushrooms & sauté for 3 minutes, or till the mushrooms release their juices & shrink by half.

3. Add the cornstarch-wine mixture & nutritional yeast. Simmer, stirring, till the mixture begins to thicken, about 3 minutes. Add the salt & season with pepper, adding water as necessary to thin the gravy.

4. Cook 2 min. More, after which serve.

INFUSED OLIVE OIL

¼ C. Mixed dried herbs, dried chile peppers, dried lemon peel, peppercorns, or a combination

1 C. Extra-virgin olive oil

1. In a clean, dry bottle, add the dried ingredients, followed by the oil.

2. Coat with a pourable spout & let infuse for 24 hours before using.

3. Store in a cool, dry place.

NACHO SAUCE

1 tsp extra-virgin olive oil

1 small onion, minced

1 garlic clove, minced

½ tsp ground cumin

2 tsp cornstarch, dissolved in 1 C. Water

2 Tbsp nutritional yeast

½ tsp salt

2 small fingerling or waxy potatoes, peeled, roughly chopped, & steamed for 10 minutes

1 chipotle pepper in adobo sauce, seeded & minced

juice of ½ lemon

1. In a medium saucepan over medium heat, add the oil & onion. Sauté, stirring, for 5 minutes.

2. Add the garlic & cumin. Cook 2 min. More, & after which add the cornstarch-water mixture. Simmer, stirring, for 5 minutes.

3. Add the nutritional yeast & salt. Simmer 5 min. More, stirring occasionally.

4. Take away from the heat.

5. Add the potatoes, chipotle pepper, & lemon juice. Utilizing an immersion or standard blender, purée till smooth & silky.

6. Return to the heat, & simmer lightly 5 min. Before ladling over tortilla chips, steamed veggies, or pasta.

HERB DRESSING

1 ripe avocado, peeled, pitted, & sliced

1 garlic clove, minced

1 C. Fresh herbs, such as dill, basil, or cilantro, washed & firmly packed

1 Tbsp olive oil

juice of ½ lemon

salt, to taste

Using an immersion blender or standard blender, purée all the ingredients till smooth. If the dressing is too thick, thin with the juice from the remaining lemon half. Serve immediately.

VINAIGRETTE

¼ C. Olive oil

1 Tbsp dijon mustard

1 Tbsp vegan mayonnaise

2 Tbsp champagne vinegar or red wine vinegar

½ tsp maple syrup

1 garlic clove

salt

Using an immersion blender or regular blender, mix all the ingredients till smooth. Serve immediately.

CREAMY ARTICHOKE PIZZA

1 20-minute pizza dough

2 C. Frozen, canned, or jarred artichoke hearts

3 Tbsp cashew crème , thinned with ¼ C. Non-dairy milk

4 garlic cloves, minced

1 tsp oregano

1 tsp salt

freshly ground black pepper

red pepper flakes

almond parmesan

1. Heat up oven to 425°F.

2. Roll the 20-minute pizza dough out onto a lightly oiled pizza pan.

3. In a food processor, mix the artichoke hearts, cashew crème, garlic, oregano, & salt. Pulse till just about smooth, leaving a few chunks.

4. Spread mixture over the dough & bake for 30 minutes. To serve, dust with the black pepper & red pepper flakes & dash with almond parmesan.

PASTA WITH VEGETABLES

tagliatelle for 2 people

2 Tbsp olive oil, divided

1 garlic clove, thinly sliced

1 can artichoke hearts, rinsed, drained, & roughly chopped

1 C. Green olives, rinsed, pitted, & sliced in half lengthwise

1 Tbsp lemon juice

½ C. Toasted almonds

2 Tbsp Italian parsley, roughly chopped

salt

freshly ground black pepper

1. Cook the pasta till al dente, after which rinse & set aside.

2. Meanwhile, in a medium-size saucepan over medium heat, add 1 Tbsp olive oil & the garlic. Let cook for 1 minute, stirring. Add the artichoke hearts & olives, & cook for 2 min. More.

3. Add the pasta to the pan, & add the remaining 1 Tbsp olive oil. Mix to cover the pasta with the olive oil–artichoke mixture, after which add the lemon juice & toss. Take away from the heat.

4. To serve, coat each serving with the toasted almonds & Italian parsley, & season with salt & freshly ground black pepper to taste.

ZESTY PIZZA

1 20-minute pizza dough

3 Tbsp cashew crème

zest of 1 lemon

1 big heirloom tomato, thinly sliced

¼ C. Fresh basil, thinly sliced

1. Heat up oven to 425°F.

2. Roll out the 20-minute pizza dough onto a lightly oiled pizza pan.

3. Spread the cashew crème over the pizza, after which dash the zest evenly over the top.

4. Lay the tomato slices in a single layer over the pizza.

5. Bake on the coat rack in the oven for 30 minutes.

6. Take away from the oven, coat with the basil, & serve.

NUTTY FUDGE

2 Tbsp vegan margarine or coconut oil

1 C. Powdered sugar

pinch salt

¼ C. Cocoa powder

1 tsp vanilla extract

2 Tbsp non-dairy milk

2 Tbsp roughly chopped walnuts or almonds

1. In a small bowl over a pot of simmering water, add the margarine, sugar, salt, cocoa powder, vanilla, & milk. Mix till smooth & well-blended.

2. Add the nuts & take away from the heat.

3. Quickly spoon the mixture right into your mold & cool till solid.

RUSTIC TARTE TATIN

1 apple, peeled, cored, & thinly sliced

1 tsp vegan margarine

1 Tbsp sugar

½ tsp ground cinnamon

2 Tbsp water

pinch salt

1 sheet puff pastry, thawed & cut right into two 3- by 5-inch rectangles

1. Heat up the oven to 400°F.

2. In a small saucepan over medium heat, add the apple slices, margarine, sugar, cinnamon, water, & salt. Simmer, covered, for 5 minutes, or till the apples are soft. Take away from the heat.

3. On a parchment-lined baking sheet, arrange the puff pastry sheets & coat with the apple mixture.

4. Bake for 15 minutes, or till the dough has puffed up & the apples are golden.

5. Serve warm or cool.

CHOCOLATE MACAROONS

1 C. Shredded coconut

2 Tbsp all-purpose flour

¼ C. Sugar

2 tsp agave nectar

½ tsp vanilla extract

pinch salt

2 Tbsp non-dairy milk, plus 2 teaspoons, divided

¼ C. Dark chocolate chips

1. Heat up the oven to 350°F.

2. In a medium bowl, mix the coconut, flour, sugar, agave nectar, vanilla, salt, & 2 Tbsp milk to form a thick dough.

3. Utilizing your hands, form the dough right into six small balls.

4. On a parchment-lined baking sheet, lightly place the macaroons, giving each a bit of breathing room. Bake for 10 minutes, after which take away from the oven.

5. Whereas the macaroons cool, place a heat-proof bowl over a small saucepan of simmering water. Add the chocolate chips & remaining 2 tsp non-dairy milk, stirring regularly till melted.

6. To serve, dip half of each macaroon in the chocolate & return to the parchment paper to cool before eating.

CARROT CAKE

for the frosting

½ C. Cashew crème

1 Tbsp powdered sugar

zest of ½ lemon

for the cake

2 carrots, shredded

6 dates, pitted

2 Tbsp roughly chopped walnuts

2 Tbsp shredded coconut

½ tsp ground cinnamon

1 tsp vanilla

pinch salt

to make the frosting

in a small bowl, mix the cashew crème, powdered sugar, & lemon zest. Mix to combine.

to make the cake

1. In a food processor, pulse the carrots, dates, walnuts, coconut, cinnamon, vanilla, & salt till a thick dough is formed. Press the mixture right into your mold of choice—a muffin tin with a strip of parchment paper works well—and cool to firm up.

2. To serve, take away the mini cakes from their molds, plate, & coat with frosting.

MEDJOOL TRUFFLES

10 medjool dates, pitted

2 Tbsp cocoa powder, plus extra for rolling

1 tsp coconut oil

½ tsp vanilla

pinch salt

1. In a food processor, pulse all the ingredients together to form a thick paste.

2. Roll right into balls.

3. Roll in cocoa powder & cool to firm up before serving.

BANANA SPLIT PARFAIT

¼ C. Dark chocolate chips

1 Tbsp non-dairy milk

1 C. Cashew crème, blended with 1 Tbsp agave or powdered sugar

1 banana, thinly sliced

2 Tbsp roughly chopped toasted walnuts

shredded coconut

1. Place a heat-proof bowl over a small saucepan of simmering water. Add the chocolate chips & non-dairy milk, stirring regularly till melted.

2. Whereas the chocolate melts, spoon 1 Tbsp of the sweetened cashew crème right into each glass. Coat with a layer of banana, followed by an additional layer of crème. Repeat, finishing with a layer of crème.

3. Spoon the chocolate sauce over the top, add the nuts & coconut. Serve immediately.

TIRAMISU

devoured immediately.

¼ C. Dark chocolate chips

1 Tbsp non-dairy milk

10 speculoos cookies, lightly crushed

2 Tbsp strong coffee, cooled

1 C. Cashew crème , blended with 1 Tbsp agave or powdered sugar

ground cinnamon, for dusting

1. Place a heat-proof bowl over a small saucepan of simmering water. Add the chocolate chips & non-dairy milk, stirring regularly till melted.

2. Whereas the chocolate melts, spoon a heaping Tbsp of speculoos cookies right into each glass, followed by a tsp of coffee. Coat with a tsp of chocolate chips & a big dollop of cashew crème. Repeat, finishing with cashew crème.

3. To serve, dust with cinnamon.

AMARETTO MOUSSE

¼ C. Dark chocolate chips

¼ C. Non-dairy milk, divided

2 ripe avocados, halved, pitted, & scooped from skins

2 Tbsp powdered sugar

¼ C. Cocoa powder

1 tsp bitter almond extract or amaretto liqueur

pinch salt

1. Place a heat-proof bowl over a small saucepan of simmering water. Add the chocolate chips & 1 Tbsp of the non-dairy milk, stirring regularly till melted.

2. In a food processor, mix the avocados, sugar, cocoa powder, remaining 3 Tbsp milk, almond extract, & salt. Blend till smooth & creamy. Spoon right into glasses & cool a minimum of 1 hour to set.

PEANUT BUTTER COOKIES

¼ C. Peanut butter

¼ C. Turbinado sugar

1 tsp vanilla extract

2 Tbsp non-dairy milk

3 Tbsp all-purpose flour

½ tsp baking soda

pinch salt

1. Heat up the oven to 375°F.

2. In a medium bowl, mix together the peanut butter, sugar, vanilla, & milk.

3. In a small bowl, mix the flour, baking soda, & salt. Add the flour mixture to the peanut butter mixture, & mix or knead to form a thick dough.

4. On a parchment-lined baking sheet, scoop four balls of dough, & flatten utilizing a fork.

5. Bake for 10 minutes, or till the edges only start to turn golden.

MANGO & RASPBERRY PARFAITS

1 small, ripe mango, peeled, pitted, & sliced right into chunks

½ tsp vanilla extract

¼ C. Nutty olive oil granola

¼ C. Raspberries

½ C. Cashew crème , blended with 1 Tbsp agave

1. Utilizing an immersion blender or standard blender, purée the mango pulp with the vanilla till smooth.

2. Spoon ⅛ C. Granola right into each parfait glass. Coat with a heaping Tbsp of mango purée, after which four or five raspberries. Coat each serving with half the cashew crème, followed by a few more berries. The parfaits can be refrigerated before serving, but taste best when berries are at room temperature.

BANANA ICE CREAM

3 bananas, frozen

¼ tsp vanilla extract

pinch of salt

1. Slice the frozen bananas right into 2-inch pieces.

2. In a food processor, add the frozen banana pieces & pulse. When the bananas are pulverized, stop & scrape down the sides of the food processor.

3. Add the vanilla & salt, & start pulsing again till you reach a smooth, ice cream–like texture.

marinara

1 Tbsp extra-virgin olive oil

1 small onion, finely chopped

2 garlic cloves

1 tsp dried Italian herbs

3 Tbsp tomato paste

1 can crushed tomatoes

¼ C. Red wine

1 tsp sugar

1 tsp salt

1. In a medium nonstick skillet over medium heat, add the oil & onion. Sauté, stirring, for 4 minutes. Add the garlic & herbs. Sauté 2 min. More.

2. Add the tomato paste, crushed tomatoes, wine, sugar, & salt. Simmer, stirring, for 15 minutes.

3. Serve warm over pasta.

SPINACH PESTO

4 C. Roughly chopped spinach

2 garlic cloves, halved

2 Tbsp extra-virgin olive oil

2 Tbsp raw nuts

2 Tbsp nutritional yeast

combine all the ingredients in a food processor or blender & pulse till smooth. This pesto will keep for several days in the refrigerator. Drizzle with a little extra oil if you won't be eating it right away.

Printed in Great Britain
by Amazon